Harry a...
Megabyte Brain

Jan Dean

Illustrated by Tony Blundell

CAMBRIDGE
UNIVERSITY PRESS

Cambridge Reading

General Editors
Richard Brown and Kate Ruttle

Consultant Editor
Jean Glasberg

PUBLISHED BY THE PRESS SYNDICATE OF THE UNIVERSITY OF CAMBRIDGE
The Pitt Building, Trumpington Street, Cambridge CB2 1RP, United Kingdom

CAMBRIDGE UNIVERSITY PRESS
The Edinburgh Building, Cambridge CB2 2RU, United Kingdom
40 West 20th Street, New York, NY 10011-4211, USA
10 Stamford Road, Oakleigh, Melbourne 3166, Australia

Harry and the Megabyte Brain
Text © Jan Dean 1998
Cover and text illustrations © Tony Blundell 1998

First published 1998

Printed in the United Kingdom by the University Press, Cambridge

Typeset in Concorde

A catalogue record for this book is available from the British Library

ISBN 0 521 63742 2 paperback

*For Matthew, Christopher
and Harry*

**Other Cambridge Reading books
you may enjoy**

Don't Do That!
Morag Styles and Helen Cook

Captain Cool and the Robogang
Gerald Rose

Tower Block Blowdown
J. Burchett and S. Vogler

A True Spell and a Dangerous
Susan Price

**Other books by Jan Dean
you may enjoy**

The Fight for Barrowby Hill

Harry is my dog. He's small and grey and
hairy, and he lies against the bottom of the
door a bit like one of those things to keep the
draughts out, but with legs. Harry is one of
those dogs that my Grandma calls a character,
which means that he does awful things, but
you like him anyway. And it's true, he does do
awful things, like the time that he chewed my
maths homework into a soggy ball and then
buried it in the garden. He dug it up later, of
course, and brought it into my bedroom to
show me what a clever dog he'd been. After
all, he had remembered where he'd buried it,
hadn't he?

"Harry!" I yelled, when I saw the dirty wet lump of paper in his mouth. "Drop!"

Harry put my squished-up homework on the floor and I snatched it up. It was ruined. A double-sided sheet of maths work, mangled beyond repair. I looked at Harry and he looked back at me with a doggy grin all over his hairy face. I groaned and turned my back on him. My life was over – Mrs Cartwright, known as The Carthorse because of her big feet and wild mane of hair, would trample all over me when she saw the state of this.

"Tell her the truth," my big brother Matt urged. "She'll understand."

"WHAT?" Mrs Cartwright's beady eyes
looked down her pointed nose at the dirty,
crumpled paper in my hand. "That is your
homework?"

"The dog buried it, Miss," I said again.

"Really, Christopher." Mrs Cartwright's
voice grew icy cold. "Last week the cat was
sick on it, the week before that the gerbil made
a nest of it, and the week before that it was
struck by lightning. And now this – this
disgusting, screwed-up rubbish! And to add
insult to injury you have concocted yet
another ridiculous excuse. Well, this time,

Christopher, you have GONE TOO FAR."

Mrs Cartwright looked like a volcano about to erupt. She turned red, then purple, then blue with anger.

I thought about those other excuses – the cat-sick and the lightning and all that gerbil stuff – I had made them up, I couldn't deny it. But this was different. Harry really had buried my maths, so I decided to have one last go at convincing her.

"Please, Miss," I ventured, "the dog did bury it – it's true."

Then The Carthorse went totally ballistic. She shouted at me so loudly that all the windows rattled and a picture of an Egyptian mummy fell off the wall.

"You are a stupid boy," she roared. "A terrible boy. A disgrace to the class. A disgrace to the school. Here." She pushed a whole stack of maths worksheets at me, a stack *this thick*, and said I had to have the whole lot done by Friday.

"And when you have done those," she fumed, "you can start on these."

Dramatically, she flung back the cupboard doors. Inside, the shelves were jam-packed with worksheets. Enough worksheets for every kid in the school to do a dozen a day ... enough worksheets to last until the end of the world. I looked at those shelves, stuffed to bursting point with worksheets, and I knew that I would still be doing maths for Mrs Cartwright when I was old and grey and drawing my pension.

"Serves you right," Caroline Foxington whispered to me as I was sent back to my place. "My mother is a school governor and she says that liars always get found out."

"But it wasn't a lie," I growled at her between clenched teeth.

"Oh come come, Christopher," she said, all prim and prissy. "You don't really expect us to believe your silly story, do you?"

"Stop talking, Caroline," Mrs Cartwright snapped.

"I was just telling Christopher about your worksheets, Miss," Caroline lied sweetly. "I was saying how interesting they are – not work at all really, more like fun." Then she gave The Carthorse a big cheesy smile.

"Did she really say that?" Matt asked when I told him all about it that evening.

I nodded.

"Wow, mega-creep," he whistled. "I don't think I've ever met anyone that crawly."

"She's so crawly she doesn't need legs," I said. "I really hate Caroline Foxington."

"And Harry," Matt said, looking at the dog who'd started all this trouble.

"Don't be daft," I said. "How could anybody hate Harry?"

And Harry, who always seems to know when he's being talked about, came and snuffled at me until I gave in and tickled his floppy black ears.

Three weeks later, I was still sitting in the classroom at playtime, doing worksheets.

"Want a hand?" my friend, Morris, asked.

"I thought you were playing football."

"Hurt my foot. I could do some of those for you, if you like."

"Better not," I sighed. "If The Carthorse found out, we'd both be in trouble."

Morris glanced at the worksheets. "Mental arithmetic. Ugh! That's the worst. It's not so bad when you can work it out on paper first. I hate stuff you have to do in your head."

"Funny," I said. "I used to think that, but once you get the hang of it, it's sort of cool.

Like my brain is a calculator, you know? I quite like it."

"Have you gone nuts? You *like* it? The Carthorse has finally driven you over the edge. Your brain has been washed, rinsed and hung out to dry. Sad," he said, shaking his head slowly in bewilderment. "I mean, Chris, this is really *sad*."

But it wasn't sad at all. It was amazing. Not only did I like the maths, but I was getting very, very good at it. So good, in fact, that I came top in a special test.

"Congratulations, Christopher," The Carthorse said. "You have done so well that you will represent our school in a new maths quiz sponsored by Slick Software. I believe the prizes are quite stunning."

"He cheated, Miss," Caroline Foxington shouted out suddenly.

"Nonsense, Caroline," The Carthorse said sternly. "I was watching the whole time. Christopher couldn't possibly have cheated."

"But he must have done," Caroline insisted, growing redder and redder as she spoke.

"Why must he?"

"Because *I* always come top!" Caroline howled. "IT'S NOT FAIR!"

The Carthorse fixed her with a steely stare. "Stop this ridiculous performance *at once*!"

Crawly Caroline knew better than to defy The Carthorse outright, so even though she was dying to let me have it with both barrels, she just had to sit down and shut up.

"You could see her struggling to bottle it all up," Morris said gleefully when we talked about it later. "She looked as if she might explode . . ." His voice trailed away and the two of us fell silent for a moment, considering that awesome and totally wonderful idea.

"Wow," I murmured finally. "That would've been *so cool* . . ."

On the day of the competition I didn't have to go to school. A long black car picked me up from home and delivered me to the Town Hall, where the other competitors were waiting. We sat in a high-ceilinged room with leather chairs and polished wooden desks, and a tall thin man with a face like a sharpened axe read out the questions.

At the end of the morning, he read out the results.

"Third place: Julia Bowen. Second place: Martin Ambrose. First place" – I held my breath and closed my eyes – "First place goes jointly to Kathy Chivers and Christopher Lees."

Yes!

"Unfortunately, this means that we are into a tie-breaker situation . . ."

Tie-breaker? What was he on about? I'd won, hadn't I? Surely I didn't have to do anything else?

"As the sponsoring company is a maker of computer software, they have decided that the outright winner will be the one who comes up with the most unusual idea for a computer game. The two joint winners have half an hour to write down their ideas. And may the best brain win!"

My mind went totally blank and my heart sank. I had come so close to winning, but now I hadn't a hope. Slowly, I picked up the sheet of paper in front of me and  crumpled it into a ball. This is where I came in, I thought, remembering how Harry had mangled my maths homework.

Then the brainwave struck.

It was like a flash of lightning in my head. Of course . . . Harry!

My game, the winning game, that is, is called 'DIG!' and the object of the game is to keep your treasures safe from a mad dog whilst also rescuing the loot he's already buried.

You have to avoid digging up other things, like tree roots and worms and dead bodies – that kind of stuff. And at the same time you have to fight off attacks from dog-fleas and from the dog himself, who tries to chew you and give you sloppy kisses and generally dishes out a whole bunch of dog-type hassle.

The director of Slick Software came to school to present my prize. He said my game was a wonderful change from all the usual Beat-'Em-Ups.

"Young Christopher appears to be a very original thinker," he said. "A pupil for your school to be proud of."

At the back of the hall, Caroline Foxington was grinding her teeth in rage.

"Miss, Miss," she said when we got back to the classroom. "My mother says that I am a very original thinker – and she is a school governor, so she ought to know."

"Yes, yes, Caroline," Mrs Cartwright said. "But not, I think, as original as Christopher, who has won for the school three wonderful computers."

"And one for himself too, Miss," Morris said, "which he is going to let me have a go on."

"I should have won that computer, Chris Lees," Caroline hissed.

"Me and Morris are going to have a great time with it," I said.

Just the thought of me and Morris enjoying ourselves with that PC made Caroline feel ill. It was quite interesting watching the way she turned all pale green and trembly.

"Mrs Cartwright," I said, " I think Caroline is going to be sick."

That night at home I gave Harry a mega-bone and a box of dog chocs.

"He is a hero," I said to Matt.

"How come?"

"He made Caroline Foxington throw up," I said, my voice full of love for Harry the Wonder Dog.

"He did?" Matt asked, puzzled.

"Yep. Buried homework plus punishment maths equals Sick Crawly Caroline," I said.

"I don't get it." Matt scratched his head and stared at me.

"It's mental arithmetic," I explained, "as performed by us original thinkers with megabyte brains."

"You are a nutcase," Matt said.

"Watch it, Fishface, or I won't give you a go on my computer," I said. Then I tickled Harry's tummy. "I am a total genius, and Harry is the world's most intelligent dog. Isn't that right, Haz?"

"Grrruff!" said Harry. "Grrrrwuff!"